WORLD'S GREATEST ATHLETES

LADIES of the COURT

By Ted Brock

The Child's World®
www.childsworld.com

Published in the United States of America by The Child's World®
P.O. Box 326 • Chanhassen, MN 55317-0326
800-599-READ • www.childsworld.com

ACKNOWLEDGMENTS

The Child's World®: Mary Berendes, Publishing Director

Produced by Shoreline Publishing Group LLC
President / Editorial Director: James Buckley, Jr.
Designer: Tom Carling, carlingdesign.com
Assistant Editors: Jim Gigliotti, Ellen Labrecque

Photo Credits
Cover: Corbis.
Interior: All photos from Getty Images.

LIBRARY OF CONGRESS
CATALOGING-IN-PUBLICATION DATA

Brock, Ted.
  Ladies of the court / by Ted Brock.
      p. cm. — (The world's greatest athletes)
  Includes bibliographical references and index.
  ISBN-13: 978-1-59296-791-9 (library bound : alk. paper)
  ISBN-10: 1-59296-791-4 (library bound : alk. paper)
 1. Women basketball players—Biography—Juvenile literature. 2. Basketball for women—Juvenile literature. I. Title.
  GV884.A1B76 2007
  796.3230922—dc22
  [B]
                                        2006029250

CONTENTS

The Stars Take the Court

THE WOMEN'S NATIONAL BASKETBALL ASSOCIATION (WNBA) celebrated its 10th season in 2006. Led by many of the great players featured in this book, the WNBA is now one of the most exciting leagues to watch on the American sports scene. More than that, the WNBA is the most successful women's pro league in the history of American sports.

Some of the highlights of the league's first decade include such stars and events as these:

• Center Lisa Leslie of the Los Angeles Sparks slammed home the league's first dunk in 2002.

• Guard Teresa Weatherspoon of the New York Liberty hit a 60-foot **buzzer-beater** in Game 2 of the 1999 playoffs.

• Forward Tina Thompson of the Houston Comets led her team to three WNBA titles.

• Guard Katie Smith of the Detroit Shock is nails from beyond the three-point line.

• All-time great forward Sheryl Swoopes of the Houston Comets does everything!

The league's popularity is built on such stars. To set up its teams, the league held a two-part draft in January 1997. The first part focused on picking players from professional leagues all over the world. The second part assigned college players to teams.

The past and present WNBA superstars reflect the league's spirit as well as the overall talent pool of women's basketball. Here is a tribute to the speed, strength, and style of these women.

Tall and talented, Lisa Leslie is one of the WNBA's all-time great players.

CHAPTER 1

Celebrating Great Guards

FROM THE BEGINNING, THE WNBA HAS BEEN A showcase for playmakers, ball handlers, and long-range shooters—the guards. Beginning with the confident leadership of Cynthia Cooper of the Houston Comets, and stretching across the league's first decade, guard play keeps the fans pumped up.

The Comets dominated the WNBA's early years. They won the league title the first four seasons in a row (1997–2000). Cooper was the star, being named the Most Valuable Player (MVP) of the WNBA Finals all four times. "Coop" also made the all-league first team four times, was named the league's MVP in 1997 and 1998, and was a three-time All-Star. She averaged a WNBA career-best 21 points per game, while averaging 4.9 **assists** and 3.3 rebounds per game.

When the WNBA began in 1997, it had been more than a decade since Cooper had graduated from the University of Southern California. At USC, "Coop to the Hoop" was a fan chant as she played in the **Final Four** three times and helped the Trojans win the NCAA (National Collegiate Athletic Association) title in 1983 and 1984. After college, she played professionally in Spain and Italy from 1986 to 1997. But when the WNBA called, she moved back home.

Already a veteran when the WNBA started, Cynthia Cooper's (14) all-around talents turned her team into a **dynasty**.

Dawn Staley is a pinpoint passer who can make three-point baskets, too.

The WNBA announced its All-Decade Team in June 2006. Cooper was one of the players at the top of the list. Three other guards also were among the top 10 players: Sue Bird of the Seattle Storm (2002–present), Katie Smith of the Minnesota Lynx (1999–2005) and the Detroit Shock (2005-06), and Dawn Staley of the Charlotte Sting (1999-2005) and Houston Comets (2005-06).

Staley, a tough-as-nails point guard, stands among the league's all-time leaders in assists, minutes per game, free throw percentage, three-point baskets, steals, and total points.

She has started every game of her WNBA career, and was a member of three Eastern Conference All-Star teams (2001-03) in a row. Staley also played on all three United States

Olympic gold medal-winning teams (1996, 2000 and 2004).

When Katie Smith plays, she knows she has one important role: Get the ball and shoot. Katie graduated from Ohio State in 1996 with the Big Ten Conference record for career points (2,437). She went on to shoot the lights out for the Columbus Quest of the American Basketball League (ABL, an older women's pro league) for three seasons, then joined the Lynx in 1999 and began shredding WNBA nets.

By the end of the 2005 season, Katie ranked third on the WNBA's all-time scoring chart with 3,729 points. Including her ABL total, Katie was the first female professional player in the United States to reach 5,000 career points.

In Smith's 2001 season with the Lynx, she set WNBA single-season records in eight categories: total points, points per game, three-point field goals attempted, three-point field goals made, free throws attempted, free throws made, minutes played, and minutes per game. She is a five-time WNBA All-Star and was a member of the United States team that won the gold medal at the 2004 Olympic Games in Athens, Greece. Smith was traded to Detroit following

In 1979, the Women's Pro Basketball League became the first pro hoops group for women. But it lasted only three seasons.

the 2005 All-Star Game, and she helped the Shock win the 2006 WNBA championship.

Sue Bird entered the pro game as the No. 1 overall pick in the 2002 WNBA draft. In college, she starred for the University of Connecticut and helped the team win the NCAA title in 2000 and 2002.

In 2004, Bird added two more pieces of championship jewelry: a WNBA Championship ring earned with the Seattle Storm and a gold medal won as a member of the 2004 United States Olympic women's basketball team.

Bird's playmaking ability is what helped Seattle create a perfect championship Storm. In 2003, she reached **double figures** in both assists and points in a game seven times—a remarkable record in just a 34-game season.

Voters for the All-Decade Team also awarded honorable mention status to Teresa Weatherspoon. "T-Spoon" is a WNBA pioneer. She played for the New York Liberty from 1997 to 2003 before being traded to the Los Angeles Sparks in 2004. Weatherspoon's marvelous **court sense** and playmaking ability made her the all-time WNBA leader in assists (1,157). At the time of her retirement in 2004, she was one of

Sue Bird went from being one of the nation's top college players to being perhaps the best guard in the WNBA.

only five players who had appeared in all 186 WNBA regular-season games played to that point.

In both of the WNBA's first two seasons, Weatherspoon was named Defensive Player of the Year. T-Spoon's best-known career highlight is a 60-foot shot she made as time ran out in a 1999 playoff game against Houston. The basket gave the

Two-time defensive player of the year Teresa Weatherspoon shows off the focus and form that made her a star.

Liberty a 68–67 victory and forced a deciding Game 3 with the eventual-champion Comets. The long-distance **bucket** helped draw much-needed attention to the WNBA.

Guarding the Future

Who are the next great WNBA guards? Two of them are rookies—Cappie Pondexter of the Phoenix Mercury and Seimone Augustus of the Minnesota Lynx—while a third up-and-coming star, Diana Taurasi (right) of the Mercury, was in her third season in 2006.

Pondexter set a single-game rookie record with 35 points in 2006; Augustus was right behind her with 32. Augustus ended up second in the league in scoring in 2006 with 21.9 points-per-game average. She also was named the league's rookie of the year, pointing her out as a player to watch in the years ahead.

Taurasi, meanwhile, knows all about being watched. She first became a national name while leading the University of Connecticut to three NCAA titles in a row (2002–2004). She was the youngest member of the U.S. gold medal women's basketball team at the 2004 Olympics, and made the 2005 All-WNBA second team in her second year as a pro.

In 2006, she had her best season yet, leading the WNBA with a 25.3 points-per-game scoring average. Who's next? It'll be a battle between these three.

CHAPTER 2

Focus on Fabulous Forwards

THE FORWARD POSITION DEMANDS SIZE, STRENGTH, and agility—whether talking about a power forward battling for a rebound or a small forward driving through the lane. The best example, and the best player, on the list of great female forwards is Sheryl Swoopes of the Houston Comets (1997–present). Swoopes was the heart and soul of the Comets' four straight WNBA championships in the league's first four seasons. After missing the first 19 games of 1997 after she had a baby, Swoopes joined the Comets for the last nine games and averaged 7.1 points per game. Her scoring averaged continued to rise, as she averaged 15.6 points in 1998 and 18.3 in 1999 before reaching a career high 20.7 in 2000.

Swoopes missed the 2001 season with a knee

Sheryl Swoopes swoops toward the basket in this 2006 game. The veteran is one of basketball's best all-around players.

Tina Thompson helped the Comets win titles with her high-scoring skills.

injury, but returned from surgery to win the MVP award for the second time in 2002. In 2005, Swoopes was named the MVP a record third time. The award matched her collection of three Olympic gold medals from the 1996, 2000, and 2004 Games. Sheryl finished the 2006 season with 4,376 points, second only to Los Angeles Sparks center Lisa Leslie. No one in the WNBA's first 10 seasons had more steals than Swoopes (586).

Swoopes became the first WNBA player to record a **triple-double** when she achieved the feat in a 1999 game against the Detroit Shock. In the 2005 playoffs, her 14 points, 10 rebounds, and 10 assists helped the Comets knock the defending-champion Seattle Storm out of the playoffs. Swoopes' son, Jordan, age 10, is named after NBA legend Michael Jordan. Perhaps

Jordan will grow up to be a hoop star like MJ—or, even better, like his mom.

Tina Thompson, another Comets forward, also joined Houston in 1997. She was the first overall pick in the 1997 draft. Fewer than 10 players who joined the league that year were still active in 2006, and Thompson and Swoopes were two of them.

In 2003, Thompson became the second player in WNBA history to score 3,000 points—joining fellow Morningside High School (Inglewood, California) and University of Southern California graduate Lisa Leslie. Thompson was an all-league first team selection in 1997, 1998, and 2004, and she was a member of five straight WNBA All-Star Teams. She also helped the United States win the gold medal at the 2004 Games.

Soon after Swoopes and Thompson joined the WNBA, more great forwards followed. First came Chamique Holdsclaw and Natalie Williams in 1999. Two years after that, in 2001, Tamika Catchings and Lauren Jackson rounded out the list of the six best forwards in league history. The WNBA's All-Decade Team includes Catchings, Jackson, Swoopes, and Thompson. Holdsclaw received honorable mention honors.

Women's basketball was introduced in the Summer Olympics in 1976. Except for 1980, when no U.S. team went, the United States has won a medal in each Games since: five gold, one silver, and one bronze.

Holdsclaw played for the Washington Mystics from 1999 to 2004. She was traded to the Los Angeles Sparks in 2005 and finished the season averaging 17 points per game, third best in the league. During her college years, Holdsclaw led the University of Tennessee to three NCAA championships in a row and was named the Most Outstanding Player of the 1997 and 1998 Final Fours.

Holdsclaw won WNBA Rookie of the Year honors in 1999 after finishing among the league's top 10 in scoring and rebounding. In 2002, she led the league in points and rebounds per game. She was one of three players to have been voted to the WNBA All-Star Game every season from 2000 to 2005.

Natalie Williams joined the WNBA in 1999 after three years with the Portland Power of the old American Basketball League. The Utah Starzz (now the San Antonio Silver Stars) made Williams the third overall pick in the 1999 WNBA draft. She was named to the All-WNBA first team in each of her first three seasons in the league. In the 2000 season, Natalie led the league with 11.6 rebounds per game while averaging 18.7 points. Williams has played with the Indiana Fever since 2003.

Two WNBA greats wrestle for the ball, as Chamique Holdsclaw (1) and Tina Thompson hit the floor during this 2006 game.

Tamika Catchings' pro career was put on hold when she missed what would have been her first WNBA season (2001) with a knee injury. But her rise to superstar status took off in 2002, when she was voted Rookie of the Year and led the Fever to its first playoff berth. She earned a spot on the All-WNBA first team in 2002 and 2003.

During the 2005 season, Catchings reached the 2,000-point plateau faster than any other player in

A Hoops Pioneer

Cheryl Miller was a trailblazer in women's basketball. Her career was over long before the WNBA was created, but the women's game wouldn't be as exciting today if it wasn't for Miller's skills. She helped make the sport faster with her speed, stronger with her rebounding, and more accurate with her shooting.

Miller was a star forward in high school (where she once scored 105 points in one game!), at the University of Southern California (whom she led to two national titles), and, finally, with the United States national team (she was the star of the 1984 Olympic team that won a gold medal). If the WNBA had been around in Miller's day, she would have been the star of the show.

Since retiring, Miller (who is the sister of former Indiana Pacers guard Reggie Miller) has been a WNBA coach and popular TV commentator. When her college playing days ended in 1986, *Sports Illustrated* called her the best basketball player in the country, male or female. Cheryl may not be directly involved with the game today, but her dominating presence will always be felt.

league history. She was also named the league's Defensive Player of the Year. Also in 2005, she played in her third WNBA All-Star Game. In just four seasons, Catchings already found herself ranked among the league's all-time best in scoring, steals, and rebounds per game.

Tamika has basketball in her **genes**. Her father is former player Harvey Catchings, who played in the NBA from 1975 to 1985. Tamika was also born with a hearing impairment—but she never let this get in the way of her success on the court.

Lauren Jackson of the Seattle Storm was the first player taken in the 2001 WNBA Draft, a year after she led her home country of Australia to the silver medal at the Summer Games in Sydney, Australia. By the end of the 2005 season, only one other player in WNBA history, Houston's Cynthia Cooper, had a higher career points-per-game average than Jackson (18.1 points per game).

Jackson led Seattle to the WNBA championship in 2004, but the previous season is when she achieved the most personal success. She became the first non-American to be named the league's MVP. WNBA stars are coming out all over the world!

CHAPTER 3

The Centers of Attention

HOW CAN ANYONE MISS THE TALLEST, STRONGEST players on the court? Nobody takes an eye off the centers once the teams enter the attacking zone. Why? Because they know it won't be long before the ball flies into the middle and the big women battle beneath the hoop.

By the time the WNBA reached its tenth season, one name stood out among the others. Whether it was leading in the stat columns, or simply having the ability to control a single game, no player came close to matching the play of center Lisa Leslie of the Los Angeles Sparks.

At 6 feet 5 inches and 196 pounds, Leslie's presence around the basket is impossible to miss. She is graceful when she moves with and without

Lisa Leslie has scored more points than any other player in WNBA history.

Lisa got three chances to wave the flag, leading the U.S. team to gold medals at the 1996, 2000, and 2004 Olympic Games.

the ball, but she is also tough when she fights for a rebounding position.

Leslie was a three-time All-America selection at the University of Southern California from 1992 to 1994, and she received the Naismith Award as the top college player in the country in 1994. Like so many of the other women greats, she also won Olympic gold medals in 1996, 2000, and 2004.

Leslie led the Sparks to the WNBA championship in 2001 and 2002, and was the league's MVP in 2001, 2004, and 2006 She was named to the All-WNBA first team in her rookie year, 1997, as well as five years in a row from 2000 to 2004, plus 2006.

Leslie and the WNBA were about to enter their third year in 1998 when the Sacramento Monarchs made Yolanda Griffith the second overall selection in the draft. Leslie had led the WNBA in rebounds per

Yolanda Griffith's hard-nosed play under the basket helped her overtake Lisa Leslie among league rebounding leaders.

game her first two seasons, but Griffith came on the scene and took over the top spot. The former Florida Atlantic University star was a force in the pro game and the first real challenger to Leslie's dominance. As a rookie, the Sacramento center was named the WNBA's MVP after averaging 18.8 points and 11.3 rebounds per game. Griffith was also selected to play in the 1999 All-Star Game, and has been named to five more All-Star teams between 2000 and 2006.

It's all about the silver! Griffith shows off her 2005 championship trophy.

The crown jewel in Yolanda Griffith's career came in 2005, when she led the Monarchs to the WNBA championship, averaging 18.5 points and 9.8 rebounds in the Finals and taking home the Finals MVP award.

In 2003 and 2004, the WNBA welcomed two new challengers in the battle for a place as the league's top center. First came Cheryl Ford of the Detroit Shock, followed a year later by Vanessa Hayden of the Minnesota Lynx. Ford was the named the league's Rookie of the Year in 2003. By the

Leslie's Lasting Landmarks

In 1990, when Lisa Leslie was a senior at Morningside High School in Inglewood, California, she scored 101 points in a game. In fact, she did it in the *first half*. Because of the lopsided halftime score, 102–24, the opponent chose not to play the second half.

During her career at the University of Southern California (1991–94) and in her nine years with the Sparks, opponents have tried to overcome Leslie's power, agility, and shooting touch for two full halves. Most of the time, their efforts fall short.

Twelve years after her massive output at Morningside High, Leslie stirred up excitement in the women's basketball world again with a single shot. In a game against the Miami Sol at Los Angeles' Staples Center, she was already past half-court when teammate Latasha Byears made a steal. Leslie took the outlet pass from Byears and made the first dunk in a game in WNBA history.

But among all of Leslie's career highlights, nothing speaks louder than an outstanding game on June 23, 2006. Leslie became the first player in league history to surpass the 5,000-point mark for her WNBA career.

middle of the 2006 season, she was averaging more than 10 rebounds per game. Ford might have picked up some rebounding tips from her dad—former NBA great Karl Malone.

Hayden's calling card is her shot-blocking ability. As a sophomore at the University of Florida in 2002, she led the nation in blocked shots. In 2005, her second year as a pro, she was still a super swatter. She blocked 68 shots, the second-best total in the league that season.

At every position on the court, WNBA players continue to make their marks, trying to match the stars of previous years . . . and to earn a place in those basketball heavens themselves.

Sue Bird (center) is one of many WNBA players who contributes time off the court to helping kids read.

Career Statistics

Sue Bird Seattle Storm

Year	G-GS	MPG	FG%	3P%	FT%	RPG	APG	SPG	BPG	PPG
2006	34-34	31.3	.411	.366	.868	3.0	4.8	1.39	1.79	11.4
5 Years	164-164	33.4	.427	.396	.878	2.9	5.7	1.39	1.49	12.6

Yolanda Griffith Sacramento Monarchs

Year	G-GS	MPG	FG%	3P%	FT%	RPG	APG	SPG	BPG	PPG
2006	34-34	25.1	.457	.000	.751	6.4	1.6	1.29	0.47	12.0
8 Years	246-244	30.6	.509	.000	.722	8.5	1.5	1.84	1.19	15.1

Lisa Leslie Los Angeles Sparks

Year	G-GS	MPG	FG%	3P%	FT%	RPG	APG	SPG	BPG	PPG
2006	34-34	30.7	.511	.400	.650	9.5	3.2	1.50	1.68	20.0
10 Years	307-307	32.4	.468	.322	.697	9.3	2.4	1.39	2.25	17.6

Dawn Staley Houston Comets

Year	G-GS	MPG	FG%	3P%	FT%	RPG	APG	SPG	BPG	PPG
2006	34-34	29.9	.420	.427	.806	2.2	3.9	1.03	0.15	7.4
8 Years	263-256	32.4	.399	.376	.834	2.0	5.1	1.29	0.07	8.5

Sheryl Swoopes Houston Comets

Year	G-GS	MPG	FG%	3P%	FT%	RPG	APG	SPG	BPG	PPG
2006	31-31	35.8	.413	.278	.764	5.9	3.7	2.06	0.29	15.5
10 Years	259-249	34.4	.441	.326	.829	5.1	3.4	2.26	0.76	16.9

LEGEND: G-GS: games played–games started; MPG: minutes played per game; FG%: field-goal shooting percentage; 3P%: three-point shooting percentage; FT%: free-throw shooting percentage; RPG: rebounds per game; APG: assists per game; SPG: steals per game; BPG: blocked shots per game; PPG: points per game.

GLOSSARY

assists in basketball, passes that lead directly to baskets

bucket slang term for the basketball hoop

buzzer-beater slang term for a shot that is taken less than a second before the final buzzer of a half or game goes off and that goes in after the buzzer has sounded

court sense a basketball term for being aware of where your teammates and opponents are, and what is the smart play in any situation

double figures reaching 10 or more in a given statistical category

dynasty in sports, a team that dominates its sport for several seasons

Final Four nickname for the last quartet of teams in the NCAA men's or women's basketball championship tournament

genes chemicals in a body that transmit information about how that body will form and grow

triple-double statistic showing that a player totaled double figures in three different categories (for example, points, rebounds, and assists) in the same game

BOOKS

How Basketball Works
By *Keltie Thomas*
Toronto, Ontario, Canada: Maple Tree Press, 2005.
A combination of science, history, and how-to for boys and girls interested in basketball.

Lisa Leslie: Slam Dunk Queen
By *Jeff Savage*
Berkeley Heights, New Jersey: Enslow Publishers, 2005.
A biography of the Los Angeles Sparks' star center for young readers.

Sheryl Swoopes: Star Forward
By *Ken Rappoport*
Berkeley Heights, New Jersey: Enslow Publishers, 2002.
For readers who want a closer look at one of the WNBA's all-time greats.

WNBA: Raise the Roof!
By *Michelle Smith*
New York, New York: Scholastic Paperbacks, 2001.
This book offers further reading on some of the WNBA's superstars from the league's first several seasons.

WEB SITES

Visit our home page for lots of links about the WNBA and its players: www.childsworld.com/links

Note to Parents, Teachers, and Librarians: We routinely check our Web links to make sure they're safe, active sites—so encourage your readers to check them out!

INDEX

ABOUT THE AUTHOR

Ted Brock is a veteran sportswriter who has worked for the *Los Angeles Times*, the National Football League, and Major League Baseball. He has also covered numerous Winter and Summer Olympics for official Web sites, and has taught sportswriting at the University of Southern California.